GIRLS' LACROSSE FUN

by Imogen Kingsley

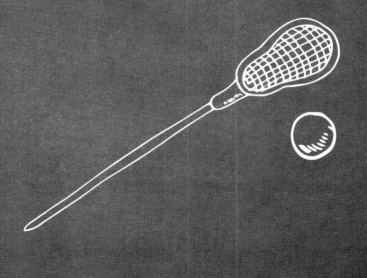

PEBBLE
a capstone imprint

Pebble Emerge is published by Pebble, an imprint of Capstone.
1710 Roe Crest Drive, North Mankato, Minnesota 56003
www.capstonepub.com

Library of Congress Cataloging-in-Publication Data is available on the Library of Congress website.
ISBN 978-1-9771-2477-7 (library binding)
ISBN 978-1-9771-2520-0 (eBook PDF)

Summary: Girls' lacrosse is a fast-paced sport! Kids can get in on the action by learning about the sport, equipment, and the importance of good sportsmanship. Then they can practice an important skill to have even more fun on the field.

Image Credits
Alamy: CSM/Rich Barnes, 12; Dreamstime: James Boardman, 13, 16, Susan Leggett, 5, 19; Getty Images: NCAA Photos/Doug Witte, 11, Portland Press Herald/John Ewin, 15; iStockphoto: iacona, cover (girl), vernonwiley, 18; Newscom: agefotostock/Aleksandr Iventichev, 14; Shutterstock: Antony McAulay, 9, CatwalkPhotos, 17, darikuss, cover (goal net), Fafarumba, cover (ball), back cover (stick and ball), 1, Haslam Photography, cover (ball), Patty Chan (background), cover, back cover, and throughout, Peter Dean, 21, Schaafb32, 6, Stephen Coburn, 7, svetalik, cover (grass)

Editorial Credits
Editor: Shelly Lyons; Designer: Tracy McCabe; Media Researcher: Svetlana Zhurkin; Production Specialist: Laura Manthe

Printed in the United States of America.
3342

TABLE OF CONTENTS

What Is Lacrosse? 4

What Do I Need to Play? 6

Where Do I Play? 8

How Do I Play? 10

How Can I Be a Good Sport? 18

Skill Builder: Cradling the Ball 20

Glossary 22

Read More 23

Internet Sites 23

Index 24

Words in **bold** are in the glossary.

WHAT IS LACROSSE?

Lacrosse is an exciting team sport. Players move fast! They run, turn, and block. A team works together. They try to get the ball into the other team's **goal**. The number of players changes with age. Games are broken up into two halves.

WHAT DO I NEED TO PLAY?

A lacrosse player uses a ball and a stick. The ball is yellow and made of rubber. The stick has a small basket called a **pocket**.

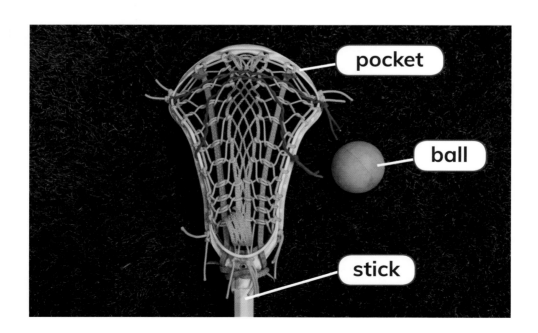

pocket

ball

stick

goggles

mouth guard

Players need mouth guards to protect their teeth. They also need goggles to protect their eyes. A helmet can be worn. But wearing a helmet is not a rule for girls.

WHERE DO I PLAY?

Lacrosse is played on a grass field. The field is marked with white lines. A goal with a net sits on each end of the field.

The field has three sections. The part near your team's goal is the **defensive** area. The attack area is near the other team's goal. The center is the midfield.

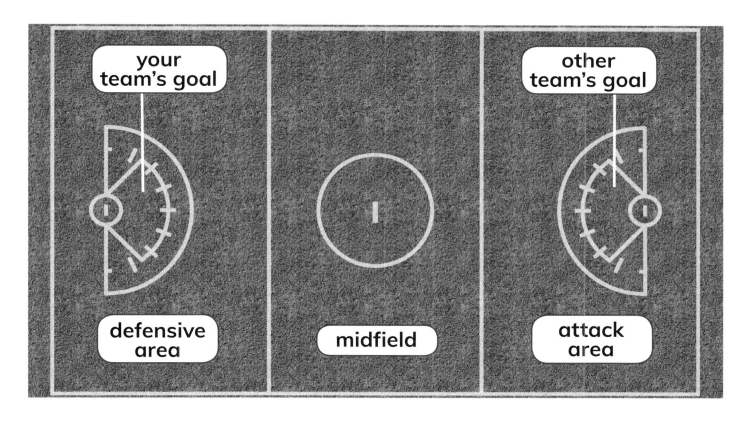

HOW DO I PLAY?

The game starts with a **draw** in the middle of the field. Two players stand facing each other. Each one is from a different team. They put their sticks together so the pockets touch. The ball is placed between their pockets.

The **referee** blows the whistle. The two players pull or push their sticks upward. The ball flies up into the air.

Players try to get the ball. Older girls can use their sticks to hit another player's pocket. This move helps them take the ball away.

Players pass the ball to move it across the field. Girls cannot touch another player's body. They also can't touch the ball with their bodies.

Players try to shoot the ball. A point is scored when the ball goes into the other team's goal.

Every player has a job. Each team has three attackers. They try to score points. Each team has three defenders. They try to keep the ball away from their team's goal.

Each team has five midfielders. They play in the middle. Each team also has a **goalie**. The goalie tries to keep the ball from going into the goal.

HOW CAN I BE A GOOD SPORT?

A good sport listens to her coach. She always plays fair and helps her teammates. She does not hog the ball.

A good sport plays by the rules. She also has a good **attitude**. Win or lose, she high-fives players on the other team.

SKILL BUILDER: CRADLING THE BALL

Keeping the ball in the pocket is called cradling. It can be a hard skill to master. But with practice, you'll learn the perfect way to cradle. Here are some tips:

Hand Position: Keep one hand on the bottom of the stick. With the other hand, use your fingers to hold the top of the stick near the pocket.

Stick Position: Keep the stick high. The stick's bottom should be near your stomach. The pocket should be between your shoulder and ear. Tilt the stick so that the ball doesn't fall out.

Wrist: Make quick, tight turns with your top hand's wrist. This will help keep the ball in the pocket.

GLOSSARY

attitude (AH-ti-tood)—feelings about someone or something that affect how you behave

defensive (di-FEN-siv)—playing to stop the other team from scoring

draw (DRAW)—a way of starting play when the ball is put between the pockets of two players

goal (GOHL)—the netted area into which the ball must go for a goal; also, a point scored

goalie (GOH-lee)—a player who guards the goal to prevent the other team from scoring

pocket (POK-it)—a small basket of interwoven strings that sits on the top of a lacrosse stick; the ball is caught and carried in the pocket

referee (ref-uh-REE)—a person who makes sure all players follow the rules

READ MORE

Editors of Sports Illustrated. *My First Book of Lacrosse: A Rookie Book*. New York: Time Inc. Books, 2018.

Schuh, Mari C. *Lacrosse*. Mankato, MN: Amicus, 2021.

Wells, Don. *Lacrosse*. New York: AV2 by Weigl, 2020.

INTERNET SITES

Beginner Lacrosse
community.sportsengine.com/beginner-lacrosse

DK Findout!: Lacrosse
www.dkfindout.com/us/sports/lacrosse

US Lacrosse: Youth
www.uslacrosse.org/players/youth

INDEX

attackers, 16

coaches, 18
cradling, 20

defenders, 16
draws, 10

fields, 8, 10, 14

goalies, 17
goals, 4, 8, 15, 16, 17
goggles, 7
good sports, 18–19

halves, 4
helmets, 7

midfielders, 17
mouth guards, 7

number of players, 4

passing, 14
pockets, 6, 10, 13, 20
points, 15, 16

referees, 12
rules, 7, 14, 19

shooting, 15
sticks, 6, 10, 12, 13, 20